MEL BAY PRESENTS

Castles, Kirks and Ca

Traditional Tunes for Cello From Scotland and Ireland

by Abby Newton

Downloadable audio files and CDs are available for the tunes in this book.
Please visit www.abbynewton.com.

1 2 3 4 5 6 7 8 9 0

Visit us on the Web at www.melbay.com — E-mail us at email@melbay.com

Introduction

In the spring of 2000, I traveled to Edinburgh to record the CD *Castles, Kirks and Caves*. My goal was to perform and record traditional Scottish music from the 18th Century at historical locations, taking advantage of the natural acoustical quality of each space. Many of the tunes selected for this project have histories specifically linked to the places I visited (for a detailed description, see the CKC liner notes). A new trio, called "Ferintosh", evolved out of the recording sessions featuring David Greenberg on fiddle, Kim Robertson on Celtic harp and myself on cello. Most of the tunes that I chose for this collection are from *Castles Kirks* and *Caves* and *Ferintosh*, which was recorded in 2003.

Because the cello is primarily viewed as a classical instrument, folk music enthusiasts might be surprised to hear it played in traditional music. From the late 17th to early 19th centuries, however, it was common to encounter the cello, along with the violin, at country-dances and at chamber recitals. In those days, the line between serious music and popular entertainment was not so strictly drawn as it is now. In fact, musicians often moved freely between idioms. James Oswald, a prominent Scottish composer of the 18th century, is an interesting example.

Oswald was a cellist, fiddler, dance instructor, composer and music editor. A "serious" Baroque musician, he composed *The Airs for the Seasons (1747)*, ninety-six three-minute sonatas for a treble instrument with figured bass. In his *Second Collection of Curious Scots Tunes* he composed Baroque settings for folk melodies and some of his own compositions. I have included selections from both of these volumes here.

In my search for tunes that are fun to play on the cello, I have perused many of the well know Scottish and Irish Traditional tune books including; *The Airs and Melodies of Scotland and The Isles (1745)* by Capt. Simon Fraser, *A Collection of Highland Vocal Airs,* by Patrick McDonald, *The Athol Collection (1884), O'Neill's Music of Ireland,* several volumes of James Oswald's *Caledonian Pocket Companion,* and several volumes of Niel Gow's *Complete Repository of Original Scots Slow Strathspeys and Dances.* Many tunes have come from colleagues, friends, and from listening to numerous CDs. When putting together sets for the *Ferintosh* recording, David, Kim, and I each brought ideas to the sessions.

I have organized the book in three parts: Tunes, Sets, and Duos. The first part, Tunes, contains an assortment of twenty-eight tunes from various sources, which are among my current favorites. The second part, Sets, consists of several tunes played in succession. Part three, Duos, includes two part scores that come from Burk Thumoth, James Oswald, Niel Gow and Simon Fraser. Because many of the tunes in the sections below appear in several volumes of Scottish music I have not listed the origin of each one separately. These transcriptions are either taken directly from the original source or are my own interpretation.

Suggested bowings and chords are marked in the scores as a general reference. My interpretations of the tunes are constantly changing and therefore the bowings also change. Chords, of course, are also interpretive, and the harmony reflected by the chords is only a starting point. I encourage accompanists to add their own chords, chord substitutions, inversions and counter melodies.

Before reading the music I suggest listening to the tune (when possible) to gain a general understanding of its style. This makes the written music easier to interpret. I am a proponent of learning traditional music by ear. In fact, when I learn a new tune that I have discovered in a book, I will often play it to a tape recorder and then learn it aurally from my own recording. When a tune has been committed to memory by ear, one can truly begin to explore it and interpretation will flow more naturally.

Downloadable audio files and the CDs *Castles, Kirks and Caves* and *Ferintosh* can be ordered from www.abbynewton.com.

About the Author

Abby Newton is well known for her groundbreaking work in the revival of the cello in American and Scottish traditional music. She first brought her cello into the folk music scene in the mid 1970's as a member of the *Putnam String County Band* performing with Jay Ungar, Lyn Hardy, and John Cohen of the *New Lost City Ramblers,* making it the first modern string band with a cello.

Abby's partnership with Scottish singer Jean Redpath introduced her to the music of the British Isles. They toured the US and Scotland and made 16 albums together. At the same time, she began an active recording career. She has produced and performed on over a hundred folk recordings, including CD's with Jay Ungar and Molly Mason, Priscilla Herdman, Al Petteway, Bonnie Rideout, and a video with Kate and Anna McGarrigle.

In 1997, Abby's first solo recording of new and traditional Scottish and Irish music, *Crossing to Scotland,* brought the cello front and center. After releasing this CD she formed a band, "Celtic Crossing", which performed the traditional music of Scotland, Ireland and New England.

Her second recording, *Castles, Kirks, and Caves,* includes 18th Century Scottish traditional and Baroque music recorded on location in the ancient spaces of Scotland. The trio, "Ferintosh", emerged from those recording sessions. This ensemble features Abby on cello, David Greenberg on fiddle and Kim Robertson on Celtic harp. Their first CD *Ferintosh,* showcased the dramatic range of color that characterizes their sound.

In 2000, Abby was featured by Fiona Richie on NPR's *The Thistle and Shamrock.* The interview and musical selections focused on her influence within the folk cello revival. She has also made several appearances on *A Prairie Home Companion.*

Widely respected as an instructor, Abby conducts numerous workshops every year on folk cello technique in both the United States and Scotland. In 1999, she published *Crossing to Scotland,* a collection of Celtic music for cello, with Mel Bay Publications. Her teaching, performing, and publishing have inspired many cellists to play traditional music on the cello.

Find out more about Abby from her websites *www.ferintosh.com or www.abbynewton.com* and Myspace.com

Acknowledgements

I would like to thank my Rocky Mountain Fiddle Camp cello student, Judy Bush for inspiring me to put this book together. Several years ago, she asked me when I would publish my next collection of tunes and generously offered to transcribe the music into a digital form. For four years she has been sending me musical copy for rhythm, bowing, and chord corrections. Without Judy's persistence and help this would never have come together.

I would also like to thank my many students from RMFC, Gaelic Roots, The Swannanoa Gathering, and The Sunshine Coast School of Celtic Music for being such enthusiastic learners and helping me decide which tunes work best on the cello. I have certainly learned as much from them as they from me.

Thanks also to Maggie Brown, Kim and David from Ferintosh and my daughter Rosie for bringing some wonderful old tunes to my attention. Additional tunes have come from listening to the CDs of some my favorite artists. It has been rewarding to introduce these lovely melodies into the cello repertoire.

Special thanks also to my husband David Hornung for his editing, listening and graphic design. He has designed the covers for all of my CDs and books.

The CDs *Castles, Kirks and Caves* and *Ferintosh* can be ordered from www.ferintosh.com or www.abbynewton.com. *Crossing to Scotland* CD and tune book are also available from www.abbynewton.com.

Castles, Kirks and Cave
Table of Contents

Single Tunes

Sets

Duos

Athol Brose

Strathspey

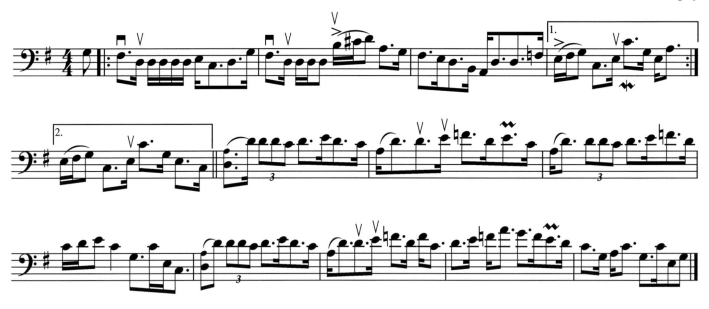

The Beauty of the North

Strathspey

Bonnie Charlie

Reel

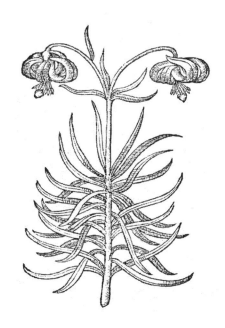

Cape North Jig

Jig

Christmas Day in the Morning

Jig

Ferintosh

Strathspey

The Forest of Gaick

Strathspey

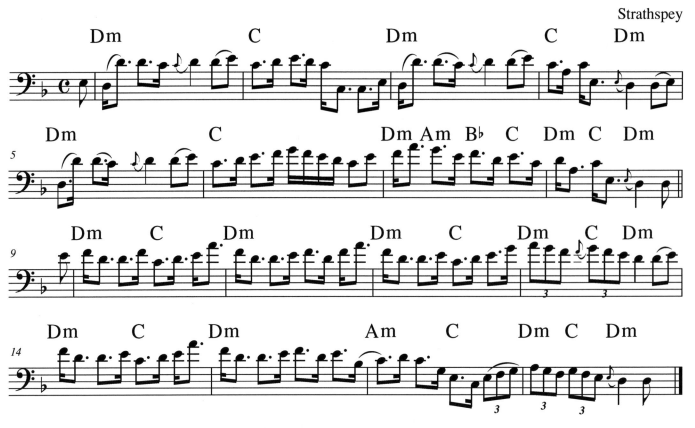

The Glen of Copsewood

Slow Air

Glenburnie Rant

Reel

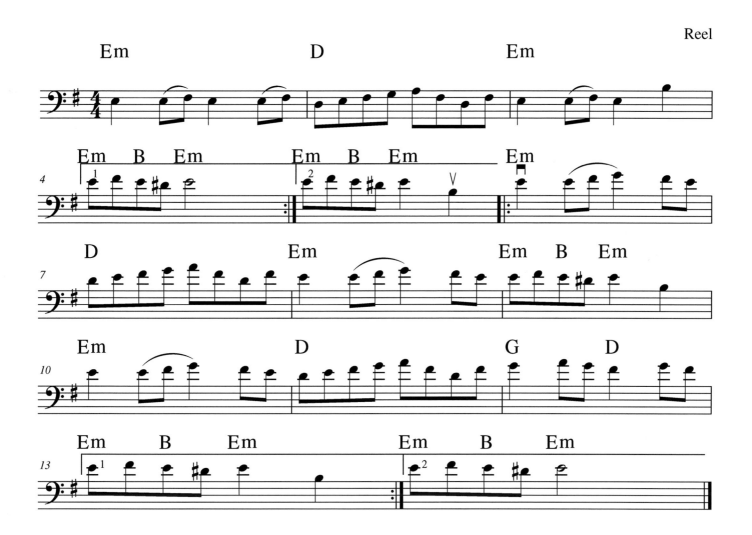

Griogal Cridhe

Slow air

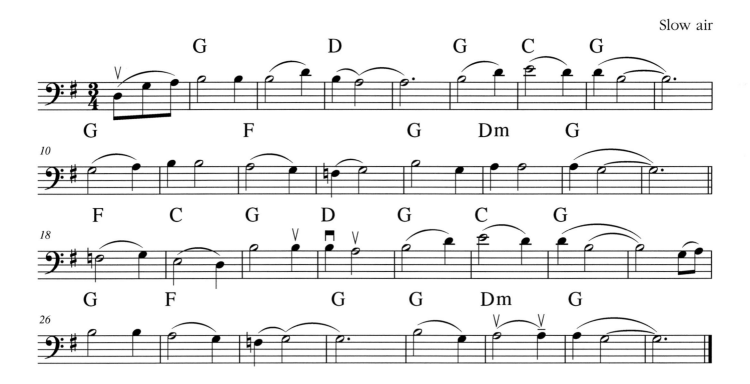

The Happy Jig

Jig

Haughs of Cromdale

Strathspey

Jack Is Yet Alive

Shetland Reel

Jessie Smith

Strathspey

Logan Water

Slow Air

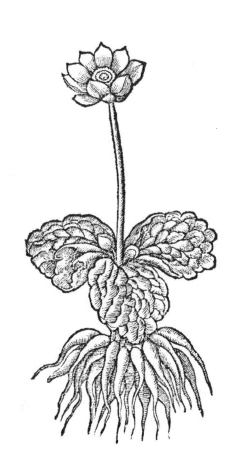

Mairi's Wedding

March

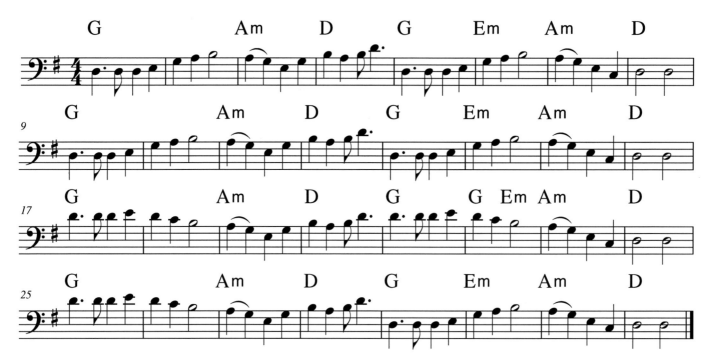

The Mill Mill O

Reel

Miss Admiral Gordon

Strathspey

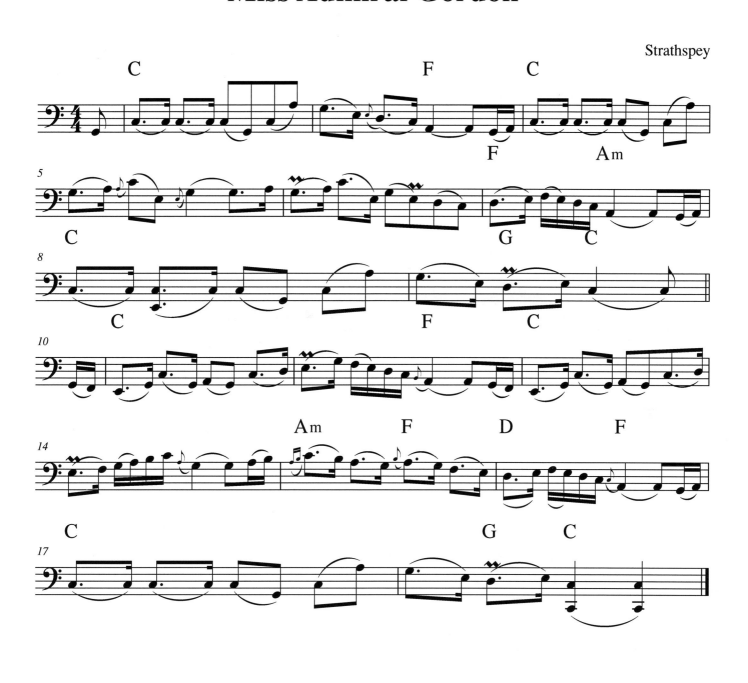

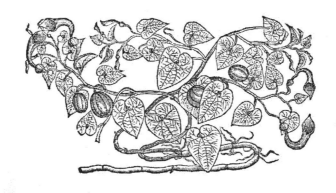

Miss Gordon of Gight

Slow Reel

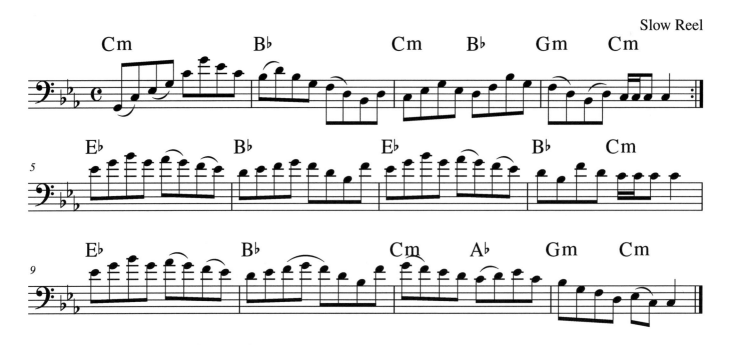

The Muking of Geordie's Byre

Jig

My Own Home

Old Grey Cat

Reel

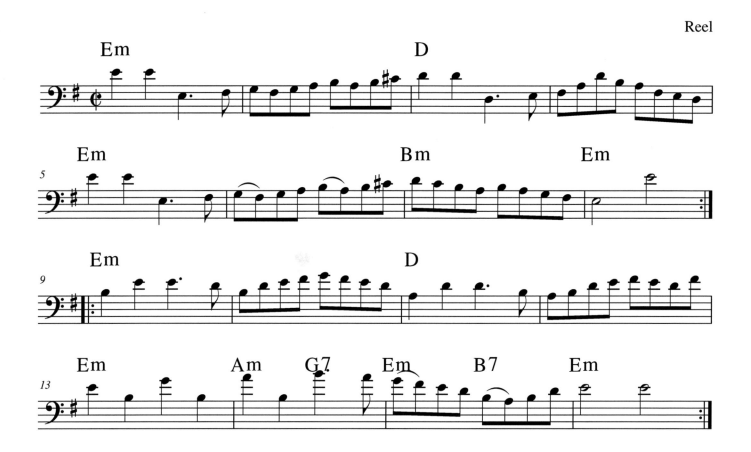

Pays den Haut

Reel

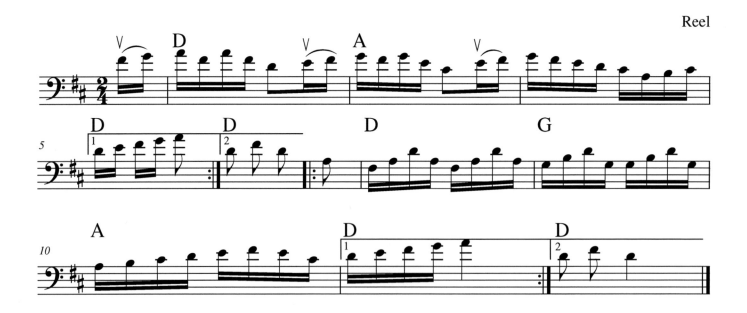

Pipe on the Hob

Jig

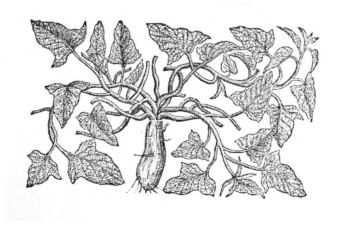

Roslin Castle

Slow Air

Tha Mi Sgith

Slow

Walking Tune

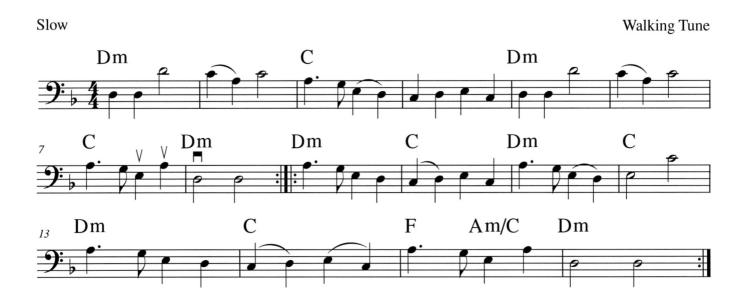

The Wauking of the Fauld

Strathspey

Ye Banks and Braes O'Bonie Doon

Slow Air

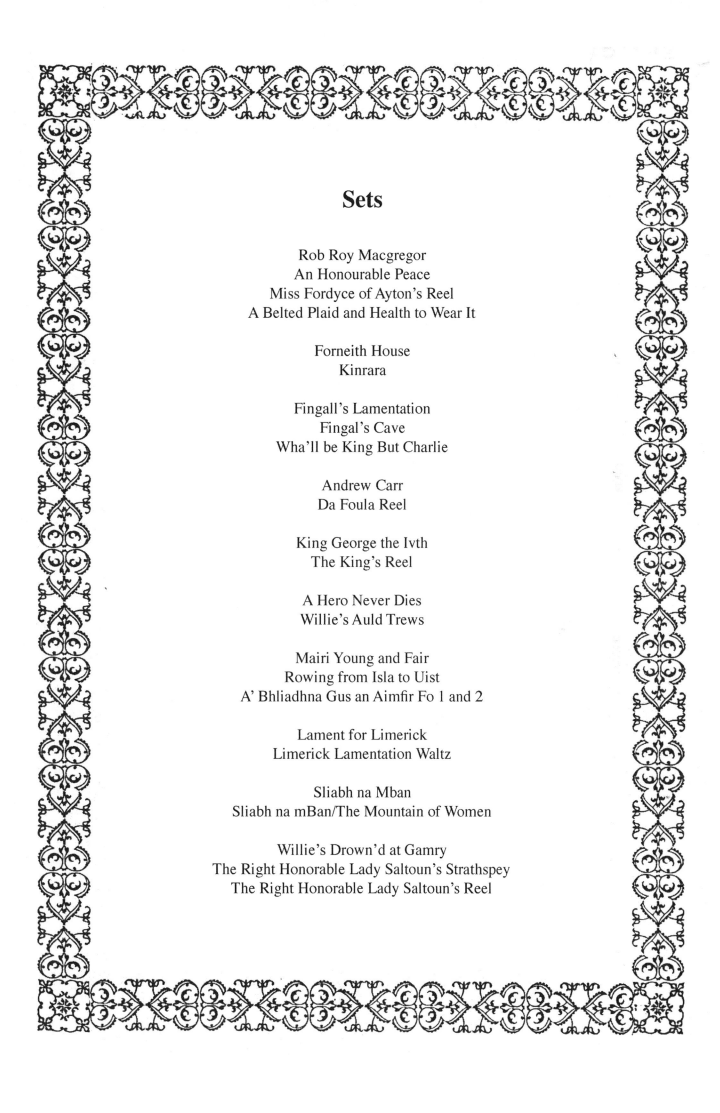

Sets

Rob Roy Macgregor
An Honourable Peace
Miss Fordyce of Ayton's Reel
A Belted Plaid and Health to Wear It

Forneith House
Kinrara

Fingall's Lamentation
Fingal's Cave
Wha'll be King But Charlie

Andrew Carr
Da Foula Reel

King George the Ivth
The King's Reel

A Hero Never Dies
Willie's Auld Trews

Mairi Young and Fair
Rowing from Isla to Uist
A' Bhliadhna Gus an Aimfir Fo 1 and 2

Lament for Limerick
Limerick Lamentation Waltz

Sliabh na Mban
Sliabh na mBan/The Mountain of Women

Willie's Drown'd at Gamry
The Right Honorable Lady Saltoun's Strathspey
The Right Honorable Lady Saltoun's Reel

Rob Roy Macgregor

Strathspey

Attacca

An Honourable Peace

Reel

Attacca

Miss Fordyce's (of Ayton's) Reel

Robert Mackintosh

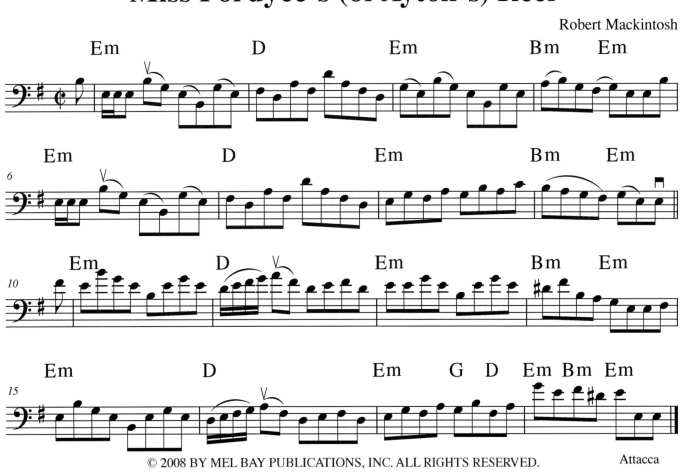

Attacca

The Belted Plaid and Health to Wear It

Reel

Forneth House

Slow Air

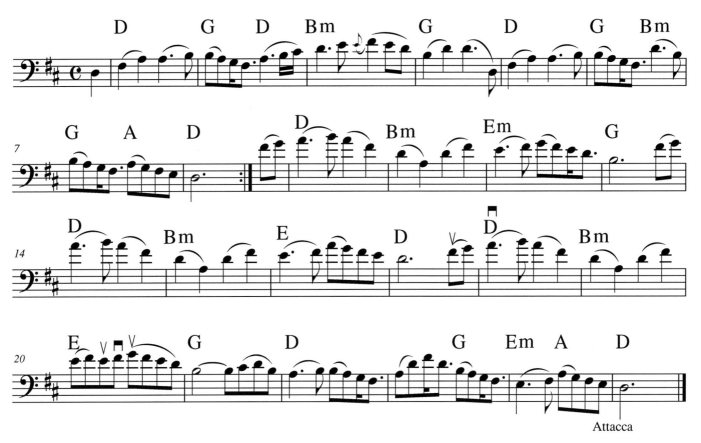

Attacca

Kinrara

Reel

Fingall's Lamentation

Slow air

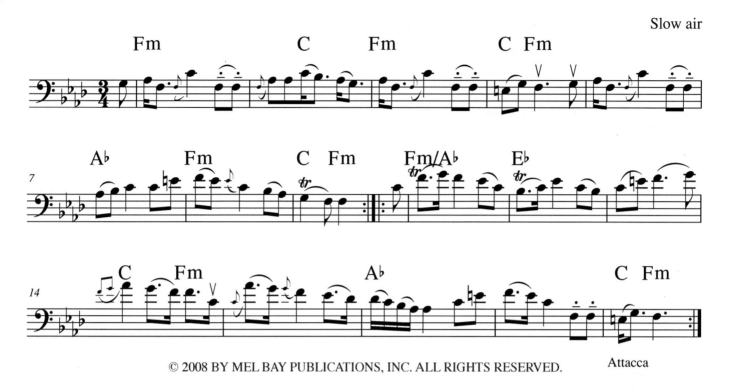

Attacca

Fingal's Cave

March

Attacca

Wha'll Be King but Charley

Jig

Andrew Carr

Slip Jig

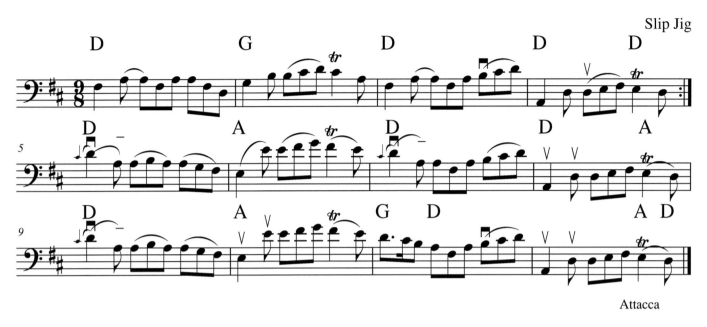

Attacca

Da Foula Reel

Jig

King George the IVth

Strathspey

The King's Reel

Reel

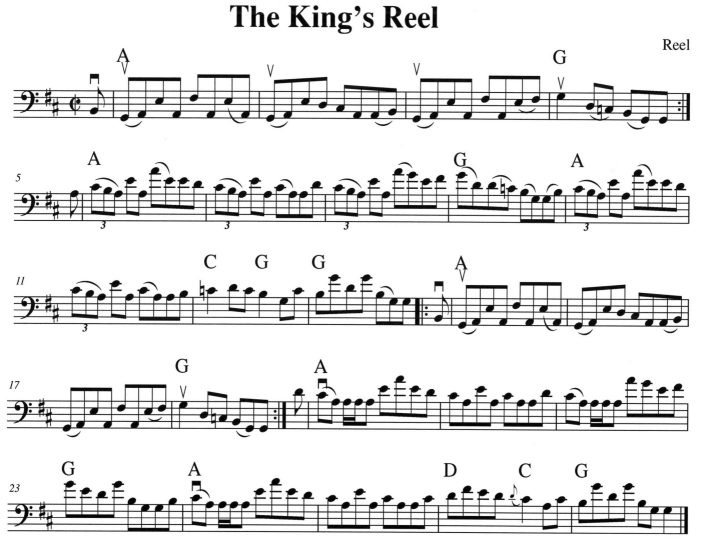

A Hero Never Dies

Cha Bhàs thig air Laoch ach cadal

Slow Air

Attacca

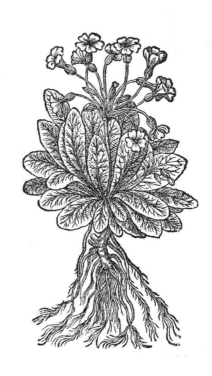

Willies Auld Trews

Mairi Young and Fair

Slow Air

Attacca

Rowing from Isla to Uist

Jig

Attacca

A' Bhliadhna Gus an Aimfir Fo

(New Year's Tunes)

Jig

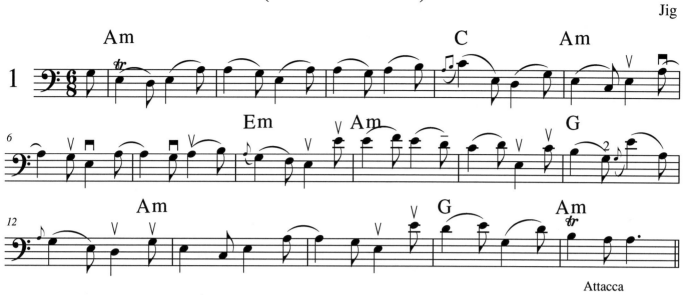

Attacca

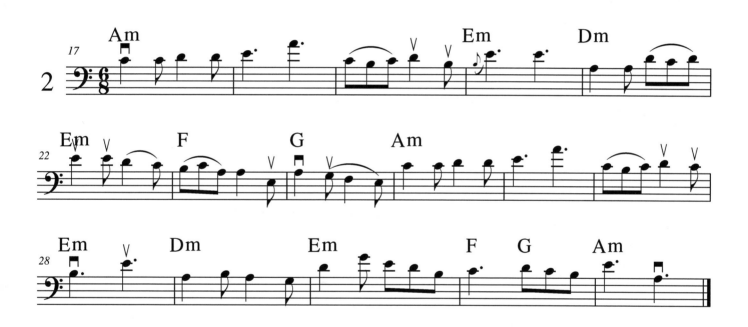

Lament for Limerick

Lament

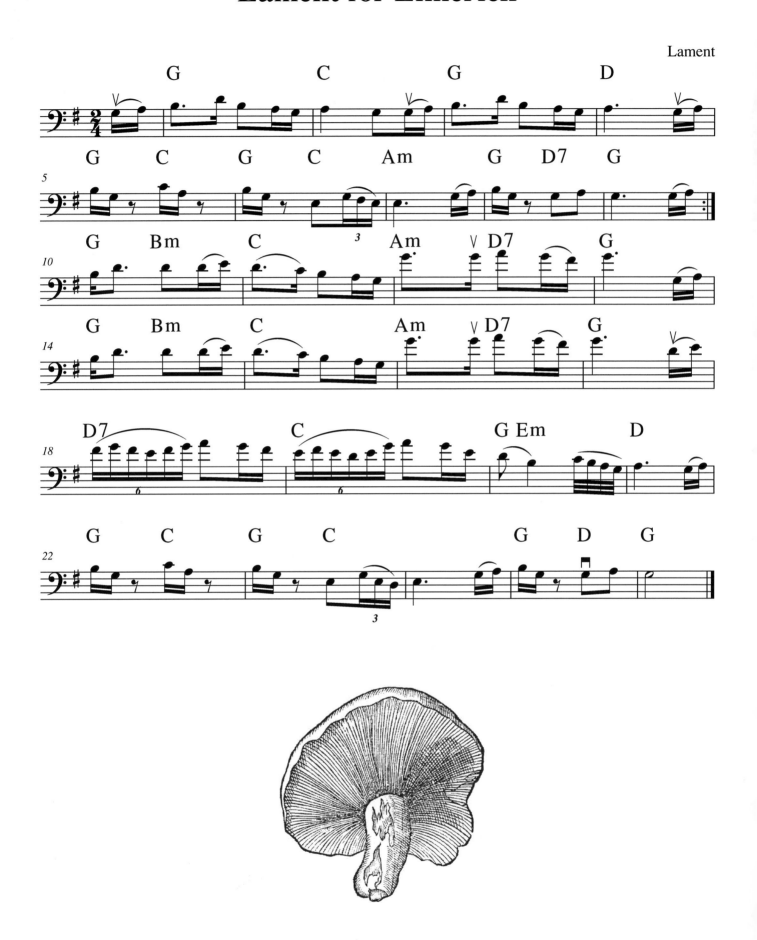

Limerick Lamentation Waltz

Waltz

Sliabh na mBan
The Mountain of Women

Slow air

Sliabh na mBan

Reel

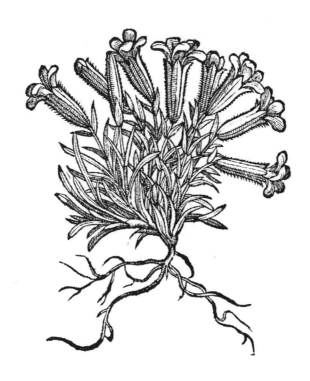

Willies Drown'd at Gamry

William Christie
Slow air

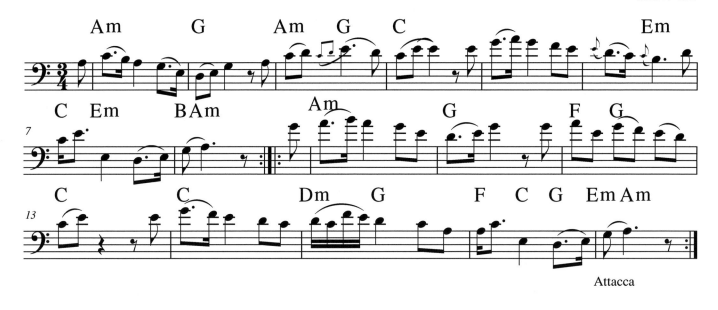

Attacca

The Right Honorable Lady Saltoun's Strathspey

Strathspey

Attacca

The Right Honorable Lady Saltoun's Reel

Reel

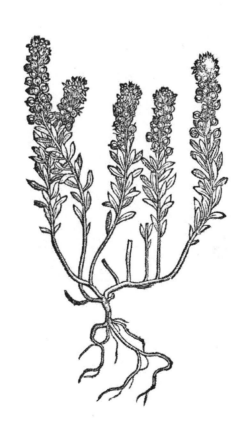

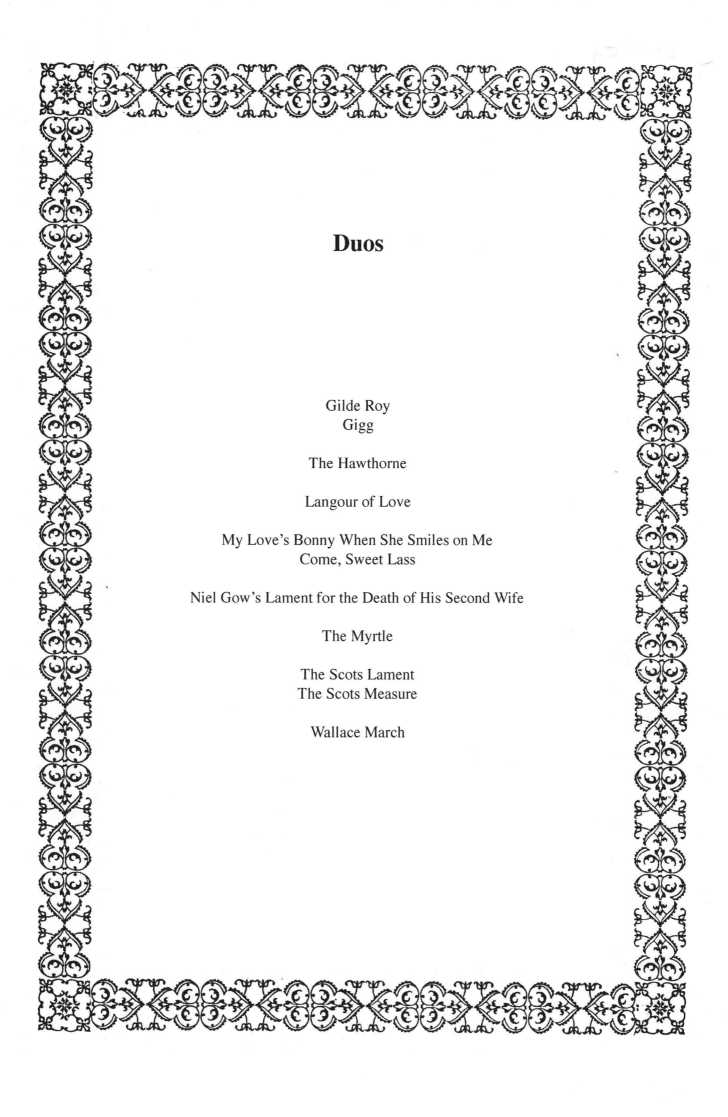

Duos

Gilde Roy
Gigg

The Hawthorne

Langour of Love

My Love's Bonny When She Smiles on Me
Come, Sweet Lass

Niel Gow's Lament for the Death of His Second Wife

The Myrtle

The Scots Lament
The Scots Measure

Wallace March

Guilde Roy

James Oswald
*A Second Collection of
Curious Scots Tunes*

Optional cello melody

Attacca

Gigg

The Hawthorne

James Oswald
Airs for the Seasons

Langour of Love

Simon Fraser
Collection
Slow Air

Optional cello melody

My Love's Bonny When She Smiles on Me

James Oswald
A Second Collection of
Curious Scots Tunes

Optional cello melody

Attacca

Come Sweet Lass

Optional Cello Melody

Niel Gow's Lament
for the Death of his Second Wife

Niel Gow

Optional cello melody

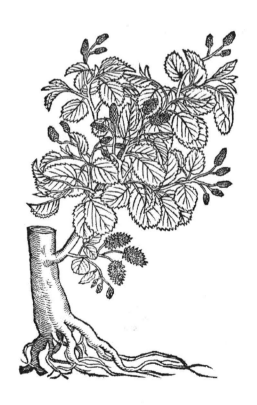

The Myrtle

James Oswald
Airs for the Seasons

Minuetto

The Scots Lament

James Oswald
A Second Collection of
Curious Scots Tunes

Attacca

The Scots Measure

Wallace March

Arranged by
Burk Thumouth 1740

D.C. al Fine

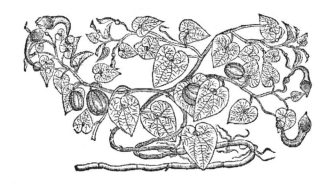